T0063582

Submarines
and
Submersibles

FIRST EDITION
Series Editor Deborah Lock; **Senior Art Editor** Sonia Moore; **US Editor** John Searcy;
Production Georgina Hayworth; **Picture Researcher** Debra Weatherley; **DTP Designer** Emma Hansen;
Jacket Designer Simon Oon; **Reading Consultant** Linda Gambrell, PhD

THIS EDITION
Editorial Management by Oriel Square
Produced for DK by WonderLab Group LLC
Jennifer Emmett, Erica Green, Kate Hale, *Founders*

Editors Grace Hill Smith, Libby Romero, Michaela Weglinski;
Photography Editors Kelley Miller, Annette Kiesow, Nicole DiMella; **Managing Editor** Rachel Houghton;
Designers Project Design Company; **Researcher** Michelle Harris; **Copy Editor** Lori Merritt;
Indexer Connie Binder; **Proofreader** Larry Shea; **Reading Specialist** Dr. Jennifer Albro;
Curriculum Specialist Elaine Larson

Published in the United States by DK Publishing
1745 Broadway, 20th Floor, New York, NY 10019

Copyright © 2023 Dorling Kindersley Limited
DK, a Division of Penguin Random House LLC
22 23 24 25 26 10 9 8 7 6 5 4 3 2 1
001–333438–Mar/2023

A catalog record for this book
is available from the Library of Congress.
HC ISBN: 978-0-7440-6715-6
PB ISBN: 978-0-7440-6716-3

DK books are available at special discounts when purchased
in bulk for sales promotions, premiums, fundraising, or
educational use. For details, contact: DK Publishing Special Markets,
1745 Broadway, 20th Floor, New York, NY 10019
SpecialSales@dk.com

Printed and bound in China

The publisher would like to thank the following for their kind permission to reproduce their images:
a=above; c=center; b=below; l=left; r=right; t=top; b/g=background

2005 BAE Systems: 4–5, 22–23; **Getty Images:** Brian Skerry 14–15c, Torsten Blackwood / AFP 17, Jeff Rotman / Iconica 18–19b/g,
Randy Olson / National Geographic 20, Kurt Vinion 24c; **Image Quest Marine:** James D. Watt 12–13c, 31b/g;
Jeff Rotman / jeffrotman.com: 3, 6, 7, 8bc, 8–9, 10–11, 13t, 30, 31crc; **Navsource:** Larry Smith / Defence Visual Information Center
24–25b/g, 25t, Brian Nokell / US Navy Photo 26–27, 28bl; **Perry Slingsby Systems:** 18t, 18b; **Photolibrary:** Purestock 28–29b/g;
Shutterstock: Idesignl 1, 14, 30tr; **SMD Hydrovision:** 19c, 30br; **Woods Hole Oceanographic Institition:** 21
Cover images: *Front:* **Blue Planet Archive:** Jeff Rotman (submersible); **Dorling Kindersley:** Jeongeun Park (turtle and shark),
Charlotte Pepper (fish and green coral); **Shutterstock:** Lightkite bg;
Back: **Shutterstock:** GoodStudio tl; **Dreamstime:** Xavier Gallego Morell cr

All other images © Dorling Kindersley Limited

For the curious
www.dk.com

Submarines
and
Submersibles

Deborah Lock

Contents

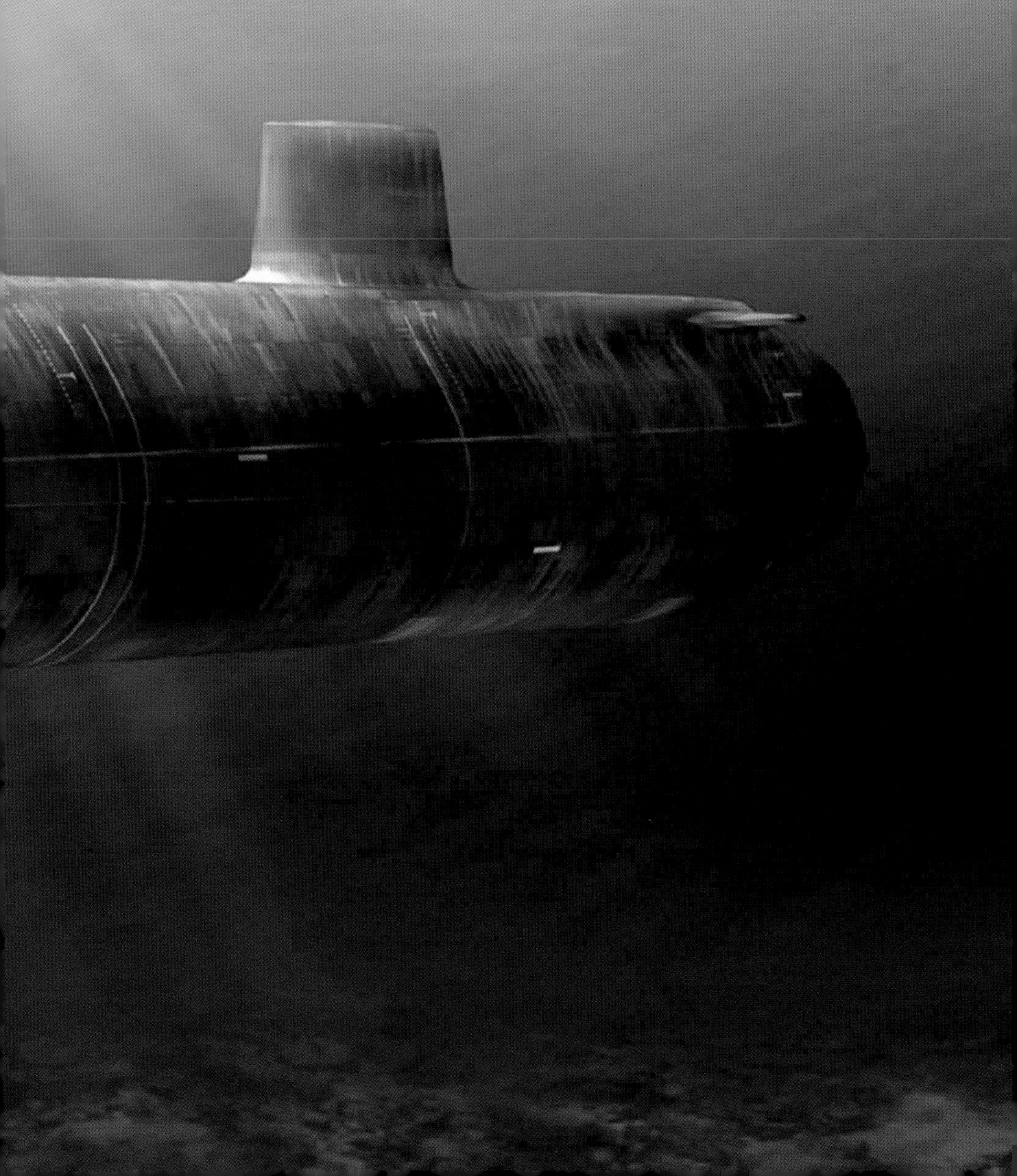

Submersibles

Down, down, down.
The submersible
dives under the sea.

Deeper, deeper, deeper.
A submersible is a craft
used for short trips deep
underwater. This submersible
has three people on board.

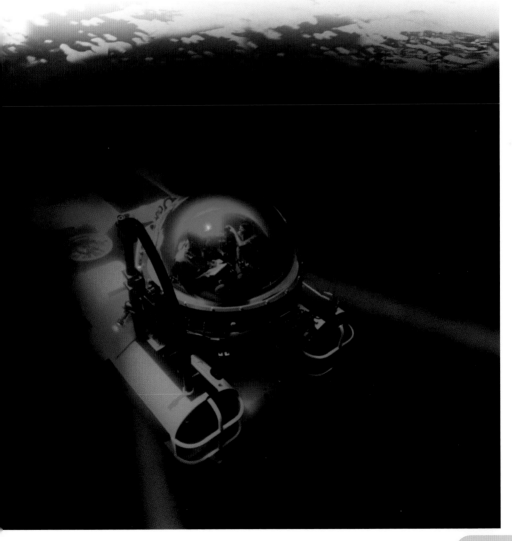

The pilot steers the submersible. The computer screen shows him where to go.

The crew members look out of the window. They want to find out about the seafloor.

computer screen

The submersible reaches the seafloor. The crew watches the sea animals. One crew member sees an octopus. They take a video of it.

They find an underwater cave.

"Look at all the sharks," says the pilot. "This must be where they rest."

The submersible moves away along the seafloor.

A strange shape appears in front of them.

"What's that?" asks a crew member.

submarine

"It looks like the wreck of an old war submarine," says the pilot.

"We'd better get going," says a crew member. "The water's getting rough."

The pilot steers the submersible to the surface. A crane lifts it out of the water.

The crew decides to send an underwater robot to look at the wreck.

ROVs

Remotely operated vehicles, or ROVs, are used when the water is dangerous. They are used to explore the seafloor and wrecks.

ROVs can also be used to lay cables and fix pipes deep underwater.

The ROV is lowered into the water. It has a cable line linking it to the ship.

cable line

The crew members control the ROV from the ship and steer it around the wreck.

The ROV sends back pictures of the submarine.

Submarines

Modern submarines can carry more than 120 people. They are often used for long trips underwater.

Many submarines are painted black so it is hard to see them in the dark water.

This submarine is docked in a harbor. The crew gets the submarine ready to leave.

hatch

Then, they climb inside.
"Close the hatches,"
orders the captain.

The submarine moves away from the dock.

Out at sea, the submarine dives below the waves. It will be at sea for three months.

After three months underwater, the crew is ready to go up to the surface. "Surface," the captain orders.

The submarine's sail appears first. The submarine makes a big wave as it rises. SWOOSH!

sail

The crew can see the coast.
They are almost home.

Glossary

Hatch
An opening used to get into a submarine

Octopus
An aquatic animal that has eight arms, each with two rows of suckers

ROV
Short for remotely operated vehicle, an ROV is a robotic submersible that people can control from the deck of a ship

Sail
The raised part near the front of a submarine

Shark
A fast-swimming fish that has sharp, pointed teeth and at least one fin on its back

Submarine
[sub-muh-REEN]
An underwater craft that can travel with more than 120 people inside

Submersible
[sub-MER-suh-bull]
An underwater craft that is used for deep-sea studies

Index

Quiz

Answer the questions to see what you have learned. Check your answers in the key below.

1. What can you use a submersible for?

2. What can you study when you travel in a submersible?

3. What can you use to study things underwater when the water is too dangerous for a crew?

4. How many people can fit inside a submarine?

5. Draw a picture of your favorite underwater craft. What are you exploring with it?

1. Short trips deep underwater 2. The seafloor
3. A robot submersible, or ROV 4. More than 120 people
5. Answers will vary